Orange
From Farm to Table

Brenda Parkes

Oranges are good to eat.

Orange juice is good to drink.

Farmers grow oranges in groves.

Oranges grow in places
that are warm
all year long.

When the oranges are ripe,
they will be picked.

Some of these oranges will go to stores and supermarkets.

Most of these oranges will be used to make orange juice.

The oranges are put in big boxes.
Then the oranges are put on trucks.

The trucks take the oranges to factories.

The oranges
are washed.

Big machines squeeze the juice from the oranges.

Other machines put the juice into cans and cartons.

Next, big trucks carry the juice to stores and supermarkets.

The orange juice is kept cold
to keep it fresh.

Orange juice is good for you.
When do you drink
orange juice?